GOD, I'M STILL HURTING

Books by Claire W.

God, Help Me Stop!
God, I'm Still Hurting
God, Where Is Love?
God, Help Me Create

GOD, I'M STILL HURTING

BREAK FREE FROM THE LEGACY OF FAMILY DYSFUNCTION

CLAIRE W.

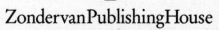

ZondervanPublishingHouse

Grand Rapids, Michigan

A Division of HarperCollinsPublishers

God, I'm Still Hurting
Copyright © 1989, 1993 by Claire W.

Requests for information should be addressed to:
Zondervan Publishing House
Grand Rapids, Michigan 49530

Library of Congress Cataloging-in-Publication Data

W., Claire, 1938–
    God, I'm still hurting : break free from the legacy of family
dysfunction / Claire W.
        p.   cm.
    ISBN 0-310-40061-9 (pbk.)
    1. Adult children of dysfunctional families—Religious life.
2. Adult children of dysfunctional families—Psychology.
3. Christian life—1960– I. Title.
BV4596.A274W2   1993
248.8'6—dc20   93-27988
                                                                         CIP

Edited by Jan Ortiz
Cover design by PM Graphics

Printed in the United States of America

93 94 95 96 97 98 / ML / 10 9 8 7 6 5 4 3 2 1

For Pesi and Herman

CONTENTS

PART I

ASKING QUESTIONS

CHAPTER 1
Do I Have to Keep Hurting?

Happy or unhappy, the experiences of childhood are usually carried forward into adulthood. Years later, under completely different circumstances, we somehow manage to recreate the emotional environment of our early family life.

Unable to see this connection to the past, we may question why we find life so difficult. We may wonder why we go from one life crisis to another, or from one unhealthy relationship to another. We may wonder why, even when things are going well, we feel dissatisfied.

Ongoing and repetitive life problems are often a sign of having grown up in a dysfunctional family. In an extremely dysfunctional family, children are subjected to severe emotional and physical abuse: beatings, for instance, or sexual molestation. Many families, however, are dysfunctional in less extreme and less obvious ways.

There are many subtle ways in which children may be hurt. They may be humiliated by a tone of voice or a facial expression that expresses criticism or contempt. They may be made to feel inadequate by a demand for perfection, or by constant comparison to other children.

Children may feel abandoned because of a lack of attention. They may feel discounted because of a lack of respect for their feelings, or a lack of interest in their ideas. They may be threatened by a loss of love that depends on their academic or athletic performance. They may be confused and hurt by an inconsistency that tells them, "I love you," and at the same time, "Go away."

For Reflection: How much of my childhood can I remember? How much do I remember with pleasure, how much with pain?

□□□

Below is a partial checklist of attitudes and behaviors that are characteristic of adults from dysfunctional families. Each item presents two opposite ways of dealing with the same issue. Some of us consistently fall into one of these extremes. Some of us alternate between the two.

_____ I have difficulty expressing anger and I am afraid of other people's anger. I avoid confrontations, and/or

_____ I am easily angered and often shout or hit. I pick fights.

_____ I am afraid of authority figures and anxious to please them, and/or

_____ I am rebellious and like to provoke people in authority.

_____ I feel guilty if I stand up for myself. I invariably back down in arguments, and/or

_____ I make sure I never get taken advantage of. I need to be right and I need to win any argument.

_____ I have to continue on a project until I finish, no matter how tired I am, and/or

_____ I have trouble completing the many projects I start.

_____ I feel anxious if I'm not working or accomplishing something. It's hard for me to relax and play, and/or

_____ I procrastinate and avoid work whenever possible. I don't like feeling responsible for being anywhere or doing anything.

_____ I'm not comfortable with other people and don't enjoy most social events, and/or

_____ I am the life of the party and everybody's "buddy."

_____ I am extremely loyal and will stick by people even when they hurt me, and/or

_____ I don't make commitments to anyone. It upsets me to think of being locked into a relationship.

_____ I am very hard on myself. I criticize myself all the time, and/or
_____ I am very critical of other people. They seldom live up to my standards.

_____ I never tell people what I'm really thinking and feeling, and/or
_____ I tell complete strangers intimate things about myself.

_____ I don't know how to be nice to me. I seldom buy things for myself, or take time to do things I like to do, and/or
_____ I buy things for myself even when I need the money for other things, and I do what I want even when I am supposed to be doing something else.

_____ I manage to smooth over, or ignore, anything in my life that might "rock the boat," and/or
_____ I live a very dramatic life, and am always dealing with some crisis, my own or someone else's.

_____ I am addicted to a chemical substance or a behavior that I want to stop, but can't, and/or
_____ I am emotionally involved with someone who is an addictive or compulsive person.

People who come from functional, healthy homes may also have some of these attitudes and behaviors. However, they are more apt to fall somewhere between the extremes given above.

□□□

It is often difficult for us to look back and assess our childhood years. If we suffered extreme abuse or neglect, we may deliberately suppress all memory of that time. We may deny the suffering we experienced out of loyalty to our parents, a sense of shame, or an unwillingness to feel again the pain we endured. We tell ourselves, and sometimes other people, that our childhood was fine or even happy.

In some cases, the abuse or neglect we experienced may have been subtle. It may, in fact, have been labeled love: "I'm doing this for your own good." Having no basis for comparison, no point of reference for understanding what happened to us, we assume that what happened was "normal."

Denying the truth may have helped us survive the unloving or even dangerous situations of childhood. In adulthood, however, it keeps us from moving forward into happy and productive lives. If we deny what happened to us, if we ignore our pain, if we feel that it is not appropriate for us to feel sad or be angry, we will be unable to work through these emotions and be freed from them. They will remain within us, eating away at the fabric of our lives.

Seeking the truth is the first step toward recovery. Honesty about what happened to us as children is essential.

Looking at Scripture: How important is it for me to be honest about the past and the present?

> Surely you desire truth in the inner parts;
> you teach me wisdom in the inmost place.
>
> PSALM 51:6

□□□

We look back at childhood in order to understand and deal with our difficulties. We do *not* look back in order to blame our parents. The mistakes they made were probably the same ones their parents made—and the same ones we could make with our own children. As long as we blame others for our problems, we will think like victims and remain trapped in those problems.

When we accept responsibility, not for what happened, but for how we respond to what happened, we are in a position of power. We have the power to change and to grow. We have the power to choose a happier way of life.

This power comes from God. He wants us to be well, and he can and will heal us.

Looking at Scripture: Will God help me recover from the negative experiences of childhood?

I pray that out of his glorious riches he may strengthen you with power through his Spirit in your inner being.

EPHESIANS 3:16

For God did not give us a spirit of timidity, but a spirit of power, of love and of self-discipline.

2 TIMOTHY 1:7

Suggestion: Memorize 2 Timothy 1:7.

□□□

We can depend on God for emotional as well as spiritual health. He is the source of our well-being. By his grace, we are assured of making progress in our recovery. We need only to desire, to pray, to take the first steps toward what is promised.

CHAPTER 2
What Do I Need to Do?

Most of us spend our lives trying to get other people to change. We demand or plead, we yell or cry, we play subtle games of power, we pray, or we hand down ultimatums. If only they will change, we think, then our needs will be met, our problems will be solved, and we will be happy.

In a prayer called the "Serenity Prayer" (given in full below), we ask for wisdom to know the difference between what we can and what we can't change. When it comes, wisdom tells us that, while we can change ourselves, we are rarely able to change other people.

If we are ever to make things different for ourselves, if we are ever to live in a more rewarding and happy way, we must take full responsibility for that happening. We must choose to think about and respond to life in a new way. We must make changes in ourselves.

For Reflection: Am I willing to make changes in myself?

Suggestion: Add the Serenity Prayer to your regular prayer life:

God, grant me the serenity to accept the things I cannot change, the courage to change the things I can, and the wisdom to know the difference.

□□□

Changing ourselves does not mean becoming entirely different people. Rather, it involves bringing a degree of balance to our lives. We create this balance by "toning down" certain extreme ways of thinking and acting and by introducing some new ideas and behaviors.

For some of us, change will involve learning how to be more disciplined, or more loving. Others of us will need to learn how to relax and play and treat ourselves better. While some of us may need to learn how to save money, others may need to learn how to spend it. Each of us has a different path to follow.

The Serenity Prayer tells us that it takes courage to make changes. Anything unfamiliar or different, even a happy experience, can be difficult for us. If we are addicted to work, going on vacation can leave us feeling anxious or depressed. If we have always said "yes," saying "no" can be frightening. We may actually find it stressful to be in healthy, loving relationships.

The discomfort of making changes, however, is only temporary. In time, with repetition, our new ways of thinking and behaving become familiar, easy, and comfortable.

For Reflection: Am I willing to be uncomfortable for a while as I begin to make changes?

□□□

We will also need courage to make changes if we face opposition from family and close friends. If those we care about question what we are doing, argue with us, or laugh at us, we will find it hard to continue. Because of our childhood experiences, we are easily persuaded that we are wrong, misguided, or just silly. We tend to value other people's opinions and way of doing things over our own. We tend to put aside our own interests, dreams, and activities, in order to adopt theirs.

If we are opposed by those around us, it is best to question why. It may be that these people feel threatened by the changes we are making. They may fear that we will no longer care about them. They may worry that we will eventually reject or leave them. Or, they may simply be confused and upset because the old "rules" of the relationship are changing, and they don't understand the new rules.

We can be strengthened in our resolve to change and to make new choices when we remember that it is all right for us to make mistakes. We are not expected to be perfect. We are simply expected to try, and to do the best we can. Remembering this, we will be free from needing other people's approval, we will be able to honor our own judgment, and we will be able to risk change. As we act on our best understanding of what is right for us, we will develop an increasing sense of self-worth.

For Reflection: How willing am I to trust in my own judgment as to what is best for me?

□□□

Making changes will also require persistence. Since we tend to respond to life according to our original "programming," only conscious and repeated effort will enable us to break free of old ways of thinking and old patterns of behaving. To "reprogram" ourselves, we need to repeat our new patterns of thought and behavior over and over again.

We will also need patience. For most of us, change comes slowly. We may improve our outlook and behavior for a while, and then "relapse." It is usually a matter of a few steps forward, one or two back, and then forward again. As we experiment with change, we need to take pride in whatever we are able to do, accept our occasional failures, and trust in our ability to be stronger and more comfortable next time around.

For Reflection: When it comes to making changes, how willing am I to be patient and persevere?

□□□

In some ways, making changes in ourselves will be difficult. In other ways, it will not be so hard. Having grown up in dysfunctional homes, we are survivors. We are hardy, we are tough, and we know how to "hang in there." These are wonderful assets to have when trying to grow and learn.

In many cases our survival techniques are damaging only because we have taken them to extremes. Perhaps you survived a difficult childhood by becoming highly disciplined and successful. As an adult, this may have led to workaholism, damaging to both you and those you love. Now, however, your self-discipline and hard work can be assets when trying to make changes in your life.

Perhaps you survived a difficult childhood by becoming a dreamer. As an adult, this tendency to escape from reality may have been carried too far; you may have become irresponsible. Now, however, you can use your imagination and creativity to enrich and enhance your personal growth.

Part two of this book is about the survival techniques that we adopted in childhood that no longer work for us. These survival techniques, held onto in adulthood and carried to extremes, have in fact become our character defects. But every one of these is based on a strength, on something good that we can draw on for our recovery.

Suggestion: Make a list of the personal assets and resources you bring to recovery.

□□□

To have the courage to proceed in our recovery we need faith. We need faith that God can and will reward our efforts, that he can and will lead us to the place we want to be.

Looking at Scripture: What is faith and how do I get it?

> Now faith is being sure of what we hope for and certain of what we do not see.
> HEBREWS 11:1

> Immediately the boy's father exclaimed, "I do believe; help me overcome my unbelief!"
> MARK 9:24

□□□

Our faith comes from God. If we ask him, he will increase our faith. He will strengthen our belief that, at the end of our journey of recovery we will find the "substance of things hoped for, the evidence of things not seen": freedom, peace, and joy.

CHAPTER 3
How Do I Get Started?

As you read through this book, you will probably remember incidents from childhood, and begin to understand how these relate to present-day attitudes and behavior. This process of self-discovery is the first stage of healing.

To facilitate and enhance this process, you may want to try writing. As you write about your childhood, you may find yourself describing events, ideas, and feelings you had forgotten or perhaps had never before acknowledged. If you will organize your writing in the format suggested below, it will become a resource as you progress through this book.

Format for Writing: For future reference, your writing should cover the four areas given below.

1. *The Experience*: What happened?

2. *The Response*: How did I feel about what happened?

3. *The Effect*: How does this influence my attitude or behavior today?

4. *The Judgment*: What criticism did I level at the parent (or other authority figure) who hurt me?

□□□

Dealing with your past in this explicit way may seem to be overwhelming at first, but you can do just a little of it at a time and you can take as long as you need in order to do it. At the end of this chapter are some examples of writing that may help you get started.

The examples may also help you get in touch with some of your own memories. In some cases, however, the past is so unpleasant that we shut it out completely. Perhaps, when you try to remember, you come up with insignificant or confusing material. Perhaps you just draw a blank.

There are several ways you can stimulate your memory. One is to imagine the rooms of a house you lived in when you were young. Thinking about the carpet, the wallpaper, the furnishings may all bring back memories. Another way is to look at old family photographs, or to discuss family history with a sister or brother.

You might also begin the process of writing by looking at a present-day problem. Ask yourself, "Who am I having trouble relating to today? Why am I so upset with him or her? Who does this person remind me of? Did I have these feelings in childhood?"

You can also spot problem areas relating to childhood by looking closely at your speech. The following expressions reveal a bitterness usually associated with childhood experiences. They may relate to judgments originally made against our parents. "You always . . ." "You never . . ." "All men . . ." "All women . . ." "No one ever . . ." "You're just like your . . ."

In looking back at your childhood, try to remember not only what happened, but what didn't happen: the hugs not given, the promises broken, the praise denied, the attention withdrawn.

There is no right or wrong way to do this work. You may write in brief notes or cover pages with detailed descriptions. Ignore such things as spelling and grammar. Only you will see this material, and only the content is important.

It will be helpful if you can find a quiet time and a private place in which to write. You might want to keep all your notes together in a loose-leaf binder or a journal. Before you write, be sure to pray for God to give you courage to begin, comfort through any sad or difficult memories, and wisdom and insight throughout.

□□□

Examples of Writing

MIKE:

1. *The Experience:* I was an only child (an older brother died before I was born), and my parents were really

devoted to me. But they worried too much about me. I mean I never got to do a lot of things my friends were able to do. And even when I was in high school, they were pretty much deciding what kind of clothes I should wear or what electives I should take.

2. *The Response*: Sometimes I got angry at them, but then I felt guilty because they loved me so much. I felt guilty too that I wasn't really the good boy they always praised me for being.

3. *The Effect*: I don't have much faith in my own abilities or judgments, and I feel I am not as adventurous or willing to take risks as other men. I'm kind of dependent on what other people think of me, and I guess I really don't think much of myself.

4. *The Judgment*: I always talk about my parents with respect and love, but I don't much like being with them. It's hard to write this, but I think they're really narrow-minded.

LISA:

1. *The Experience*: I was eight when Mama died, so it was my Aunt Leslie who brought me up. When I said I wanted ballet lessons, she told me I was too fat and clumsy and that it would be a waste of time and money. I can't remember her ever saying anything nice about me. No matter how hard I tried, nothing I did was good enough. And I can't remember her

buying me anything that wasn't absolutely necessary or on sale.

2. *The Response*: I felt sad about the ballet lessons, but I felt she was probably right about me. I think I never expected her to say yes anyway.

3. *The Effect*: My friends do a lot of things for themselves—like taking night courses or getting cosmetic make overs, but I find it really hard to spend money on myself. Sometimes I spend a lot of money on my little boy, but I always make a big deal of it. I mean, he really has to appreciate how much I've spent.

4. *The Judgment*: Aunt Leslie is dead now, but I still tell my husband stories about what a miser she was—how stingy and cheap and mean.

KEVIN:

1. *The Experience*: Pop came home drunk one night and yelled at me for not having taken out the garbage. When I started to argue with him, he came after me. Mom started pleading and got in front of me, but he just threw her against the refrigerator and kept on hitting me. My left wrist is still kind of crooked from that beating.

2. *The Response*: At first I was scared. Afterward, I wanted to kill him. I was up all night, not only because I hurt all over—especially my wrist, but because I kept planning ways to get even.

3. *The Effect*: I don't like it when people get angry, and I'll walk out of the room to avoid an argument with my wife. Sometimes, though, I just go crazy with the kids and I start screaming at them and even hitting them. It scares me and I feel terrible afterward.

4. *The Judgment*: As far as I'm concerned, my father is a lousy drunk. I don't think much of my mom either, for putting up with him all these years. She should have protected me and my sister. She should have left him, but she was too weak.

SARA:

1. *The Experience*: When I was about seven, I saved up money to buy a present for my father. I wanted him to love me as much as he loved my sister. When I gave it to him, he probably thanked me for it. I don't remember. I just remember he turned around then and started playing with my sister.

2. *The Response*: I was so hurt. I hated him.

3. *The Effect*: I've always been afraid that men would reject me, so I've always acted cool and distant—especially if I was attracted to someone. I took pains to ignore him. I just couldn't bear the humiliation of some guy knowing I liked him when he didn't like me. I married a really distant sort of man and when he was unfaithful to me, as much as it hurt, I pretended it didn't matter, and I allowed it to

continue. I guess I "knew" something like that was
bound to happen to me.

4. *The Judgment*: I decided my father was a cold and
heartless person. I suppose I decided all men were
like that.

□□□

Suggestion: Try to do at least one or two writing
exercises before proceeding to the next chapter. Then, if
you are impatient to read on, you can continue your
writing as you progress through the book. Dealing with
the past is often a stop-and-go process. You do not have
to rush this process. You do not have to do more than
you feel ready to do.

CHAPTER 4
Can I Do This on My Own?

The writing described in the last chapter helps us break through denial. It helps us recognize and acknowledge the reality of what happened to us as children. Writing of this sort brings clarity and understanding. Because it is an intellectual activity, however, it is only the first stage of the healing process. Understanding alone does not free us. We must also *feel*.

In the second stage of our healing, we experience and walk through the emotions we suppressed as children: the anger that covers our hurt, the hurt that covers our fear, and the fear that covers our grief.

The only way we can do this "feeling work" is with other people. In the presence of others who love and understand us, we are able to experience, express, and finally let go of our feelings. We receive the kind of "family" support that was denied to us as children.

If you were to take one of the exercises you wrote from the last chapter and read it to another person, you would probably find yourself feeling more emotion than when you wrote the material or when you read it back to yourself. Most writing is done in a state of limited feeling and sometimes in a state of complete numbness.

For Reflection: How much did I feel when writing or reading back the exercises from the last chapter?

Suggestion: Try reading one or more of your writing exercises to a family member, or to a friend.

□□□

Reaching out to others is difficult for those of us who grew up in dysfunctional homes. We have been taught to be self-sufficient, to rely only on ourselves, to trust only ourselves.

We have also been taught not to talk—especially to people outside the family—about family secrets. We feel disloyal in doing so, as though we are betraying those closest to us.

Pride may also keep us from sharing the truth about ourselves to others. The embarrassment we felt as children, either for ourselves or for our families, makes us sensitive about the image we present to the world: "If I get emotional, I'll look like a fool." "If I get angry, I'll look ugly." "If I cry, they'll think I'm weak."

Our insistence on self-sufficiency, our distrust of others, our sense of family loyalty, and our pride all keep us trapped in our dysfunction. When we reach out to others, when we ask for help, we exhibit tremendous strength. We say, in effect, that we are worthy and capable of growth. We do not betray ourselves or our families; we betray the sickness that holds us captive.

For Reflection: How willing am I to express my feelings to other people?

□□□

It has taken courage for you to be honest in your writing, and it will take courage to be honest in sharing with another person. There are some considerations, however, that will make the process easier.

If your history involves serious trauma such as sexual molestation, you will need someone with professional training to help you. Even without obvious or violent abuse in your background, you may find it best to begin your recovery with a therapist or a member of the clergy who is sensitive to the issues of adults from dysfunctional families.

Although a counselor's training is important, professional credits and/or church affiliation are not a guarantee of helpfulness. It is also important for you to feel good about the person you choose. You will want someone you can trust and be comfortable with— someone who reflects God's unconditional love and acceptance of you. You may have to "shop around" for a while to find the right person, and you may need to change your mind at some point.

Looking at Scripture: Do I need to be careful about who I pick to confide in?

> Like a bad tooth or a lame foot is reliance
> on the unfaithful in times of trouble.
>   PROVERBS 25:19

□□□

If you choose a friend to help you, rather than a trained professional, you will need a mature, loving, and sensitive person who knows how to listen. Sometimes our friends, in their eagerness to be helpful, actually make things worse for us. Because they feel distressed at seeing us in pain, they try to cheer us up. This response cuts us off from expressing our feelings and working through them. It invalidates our feelings and, in a sense, invalidates us. Our pain is only increased.

Looking at Scripture: Can the wrong kind of listener make me feel worse?

> Like one who takes away a garment on a
> cold day, or like vinegar poured on soda,
> is one who sings songs to a heavy heart.
>   PROVERBS 25:20

> Rejoice with those who rejoice; mourn
> with those who mourn.
>   ROMANS 12:15

□□□

Sometimes our friends respond to our pain by wanting

to "fix" us. They interpret our sharing as a plea for help and direction. By rushing in with good advice, they do the same thing as those who try to cheer us up: they cut us off from expressing our feelings. They may even add to our burden by leaving us feeling guilty, childish, or inadequate.

While advice can sometimes be helpful, people rarely know enough about us, or about our situation, to be able to tell us what to do. Even when their advice is from Scripture, the verses they use may be misunderstood or used inappropriately. A particular verse may seem to speak to our problem, but it may have been taken out of context, or it may be balanced or qualified by another biblical passage.

In all our relationships, the expression of love is the most important factor. We feel loved by those people who listen to us in an attentive and respectful way, and who allow us to make our own choices. The absence of advice gives us a very encouraging message: "You don't need me to give you advice. I believe you will discover the right answer for yourself. I know God will guide you and take care of you if you seek his wisdom."

Suggestion: Tell your friends how you want them to respond when you talk to them about problems.

□□□

An especially helpful framework in which to share is a group. A group can become like a family—a functional family in which the members are learning to communicate with honesty and to support one another with love.

A group enables us to hear about other people's problems. This may help us sort out and identify our own problems. Learning about their fear and pain, we feel less different and alone in our own fear and pain.

A group also enables us to watch and learn from other people who are in recovery. Seeing them deal with their problems and make successful changes in their lives, watching them sometimes fail and then begin again, we are encouraged in our own recovery process.

Still another advantage of being in a group is that we give, as well as receive, support. Feelings of guilt and shame are replaced with a sense of self-worth as we come to be of real service to others.

Suggestion: Pray for wisdom and guidance in selecting people with whom you can share your recovery. Then make a list of friends, therapists, and/or groups you might try working with, and begin exploring the possibilities.

□□□

You may be able to find a support group or a church fellowship where you can share with honesty. If not, you might want to form a group yourself. There are guidelines at the back of this book that can help you get started.

If you are already in a group that is using this book, the questions after "For Reflection" and "Looking at Scripture" can be used to promote a deep level of sharing. If your group is small and intimate, and you have been meeting long enough to develop feelings of trust and safety, you may want to try the following exercise:

Each group member, in turn, relates a sad or painful incident from childhood, something that took place before the age of ten. There should be no responses from the group to this sharing.

Each person then writes a letter to the parent or parents who figured in the incident. As you write the letter, imagine that you are the young child speaking. Explain how you feel and say what it is that you want from your parent(s). Use your less-dominant hand to write the letter (your left hand, if you are right-handed) and print rather than use script. A sample letter is given on the next page.

When the letters are finished, each person in turn reads aloud what he or she has written. When a person has finished reading, each member of the group then responds in a positive way: with a short statement of regard or encouragement, or with a touch or a hug.

Some people doing this exercise may become very emotional, while others may go through it quietly. Whatever the immediate reaction, (and there is no right or wrong way to react), this kind of sharing will eventually contribute, in a powerful way, to the healing process.

Dear Mom+ Dad,
    I needed for you
to spend time with me,
to ask me how I felt
about things, to listen
to me talk. I needed
you to sometimes play with
me, or take me to nice
places just for me,
or buy me nice things
because you bred me and
thought I was important—
as important as the other
people in the family.
        I love you
        Claire

Looking at Scripture: How important is it to share my recovery with other people?

> Carry each other's burdens, and in this
> way you will fulfill the law of Christ.
> GALATIANS 6:2

□ □ □

Through sharing our burdens, we begin to overcome one of our greatest problems: the feeling of being different and alone. We begin to feel that we belong, that we fit in. As others accept the truth about us, we accept ourselves and come to believe—for the first time, perhaps—that we are accepted and loved by God, that we are truly members of his family.

PART II

LOOKING AT PROBLEMS

CHAPTER 5
Hurting for Love

Part two of this book deals with the effects of growing up in a dysfunctional family. It may help you understand how specific experiences from your childhood influence the way you respond to life today.

Parents who love their children are not always able to express that love effectively. Some parents are too troubled by circumstances or by their own emotional problems to interact with their children in healthy ways.

Some of us grew up being told we were loved, but feeling we were not. If we feel we are not loved, we may decide that we are unlovable. We may have grown up trying to secure love in ways that harm us now.

For instance, we encourage others to take advantage of us. We may be "people pleasers" sometimes with just a spouse or family members, sometimes with complete strangers. If our gifts of time or money or love are not returned, we feel unappreciated, hurt, and resentful—but we continue to give. This is not the cheerful giving God would have us engage in. It is a sad and angry sacrifice based on a fear of rejection.

If we feel that it is impossible to get the love we need from others, we may decide to love ourselves to the point of self-indulgence. We may spend money on ourselves, take time for ourselves, and be unwilling to give anything to others. Focused entirely on our own needs, we may find it impossible to be generous to others. We may, in fact, be stingy.

For Reflection: In what ways do I try to secure love from others—or give it to myself?

Suggestion: If you are a "people pleaser," plan to buy something nice for yourself, or take some time to do something you enjoy. If you tend to be self-indulgent, plan to do something special for another person.

□□□

If childhood has taught us that we are unlovable, we may be easily hurt by anything people say or do that seems to confirm that idea. For instance, we may be deeply offended at being kept waiting for a few moments, or we may feel insulted and rejected if someone forgets to ask us how we are.

While we sometimes overreact to small or imagined slights, more often than not we underreact to serious wrongs committed against us. Believing ourselves to be unlovable, we expect very little from others in the way of kindness or respect. For example, a woman may tolerate her husband's infidelity; a man may allow his friend to belittle him in public. These hurts may be borne with little or no reaction.

For Reflection: Am I ever overly sensitive—or overly tolerant—of what others say and do to me?

□□□

Our need for love can drive us to promiscuity. The sex itself, however, may be less important to us than hugs, attention, acceptance, or anything else that comes close to feeling like love. The sexual activity may actually be unsatisfying. Sexual enjoyment is based, not only on love for the partner, but on self-love and an ability to express one's needs. If our focus is totally on our performance or the impression we are making on our partner, we will have little enjoyment.

Just as our need for love can lead us into promiscuity, our fear that we will be rejected can cause us to withdraw from intimate relationships. This withdrawal, often in the form of a complete loss of sexual desire, can be experienced whether we are single or married.

For Reflection: How satisfied am I with my ability to enjoy a rewarding intimate relationship?

Suggestion: Find someone to hug today. If you are uncomfortable with hugging, start by just touching another person's hand, or patting their shoulder. If you are uncomfortable asking for affection, look in the mirror and practice saying "I need a hug." Try to hug someone every day.

□ □ □

Whether or not we marry, whether or not we have friends, we seldom feel sure of being loved. We are often jealous and our need for time and attention can overwhelm those around us. We crave reassurance not only in that we are loved but also in that the love will continue.

As children, we may have experienced love as being precarious. A parent who was kind one minute may have turned angry and violent, or cold and withdrawn, the next. Sometimes parents fail to keep their promises. Sometimes they disappear on trips or on alcoholic binges. Sometimes they withdraw emotionally into depression, leave the family, or die.

For Reflection: Is there some way, emotionally or physically, in which I "lost" one or both of my parents?

□ □ □

A parent who fails us will leave us feeling insecure and unsure about people. As adults, a fear of being abandoned may determine the kinds of people we choose for close relationships. For instance, we may seek out friends or mates who have problems. Even though they appear to be strong, we sense their vulnerability and low self-esteem. We are attracted by their weakness because it gives us a feeling of security: If they need us, they won't leave us.

We may also try to hold on to people by taking the needy or weak role ourselves. We seek out friends or mates who are willing to take care of us. We give our problems to them, hoping that once they feel responsible for us, they will not be able to leave us.

Whichever role we take, we find ourselves involved in what is called a "codependent" relationship. Codependents assume complete responsibility for the happiness and well-being of other people. They become so focused on the problems, thinking, and behavior of others that they become unaware of, and unresponsive to, their own needs.

For Reflection: To what degree am I involved in codependent relationships?

□ □ □

The fear of being abandoned keeps some of us loyal and committed when it is inappropriate to be so. We cling to people who are unsuitable and try to maintain relationships that are unrewarding or even harmful.

In contrast, the same fear keeps some of us from getting too deeply involved with others. If we are not able to keep a relationship on a superficial level, we change partners. We are threatened by intimacy and find it impossible to make any real commitment.

Sadly enough, many of us who overcommit find ourselves in relationships with those who are afraid of commitment. We are so certain that we will be abandoned that we somehow make it happen. We choose partners who are emotionally unavailable or who are certain to betray or leave us.

Even if our partner is capable of making a commitment, we may find ways to sabotage the relationship. Sometimes we do this in the early stages, before we can become too involved and too vulnerable: "I know I'm going to get hurt eventually. Let's get it over with now." At other times we wait to create difficulties in a long-term relationship. We may be many years into a marriage before we begin to test the tolerance of our spouse and then quite literally drive that person away from us.

For Reflection: Does fear of being abandoned play a part in my relationships? If so, how?

□□□

While we need to know we are loved by others, we need even more to know we are loved by God. Only God can provide us with unconditional and unfailing love.

Many of us, however, doubt that God loves us. We have an image of God that resembles an abusive parent: angry, critical, punishing, and temperamental. We respond to that image by rejecting him or by trying to please him out of fear. When we are told by Scripture that God *is* love, we have trouble envisioning what that means.

Looking at Scripture: What is God's love like?

> Love is patient, love is kind. It does not
> envy, it does not boast, it is not proud. It
> is not rude, it is not self-seeking, it is not
> easily angered, it keeps no record of
> wrongs. Love does not delight in evil but
> rejoices with the truth.
>
> 1 CORINTHIANS 13:4–6

Looking at Scripture: Can I depend on God's love?

> The LORD appeared to us in the past,
> saying: "I have loved you with an ever-
> lasting love; I have drawn you with
> loving-kindness."
>
> JEREMIAH 31:3

> Because God has said, "Never will I leave
> you; never will I forsake you."
>
> HEBREWS 13:5

Suggestion: Make a list of all the things that "say"
love to you (for example: speaking softly to me, feeling
sympathy for me, being there when I need someone).
When you are finished, write at the top of the list:
"These are the ways God loves me."

□□□

As we progress in recovery, we begin to understand
and believe in God's love for us. We experience the
warmth and the constancy of his love. As a result, we
are free to receive and return, not only his love, but the
love of other people.

CHAPTER 6
Hurting for Approval

All children need approval. Children who are constantly criticized, teased, shamed, or ignored, form a poor opinion of themselves. They believe the negative things that their parents say about them. They believe that they deserve the neglect or the harsh treatment they receive.

These negative messages from childhood often continue into adulthood and remain more powerful than any new and positive messages. We may cling to low self-esteem even in the face of great success or the admiration of others.

If we ignore even our triumphs, it is because we are perfectionists. We set impossibly high standards for ourselves. In order to meet them, we may become workaholics or overachievers. When this happens, we are driven to succeed even at the cost of our health or our relationships.

Sometimes perfectionism creates the opposite kind of reaction. We become overwhelmed by our high standards, or by the number of things we try to accomplish. We procrastinate, lose all ambition, and eventually give up without really trying. If we act irresponsibly, it is because we "know" we are going to fail.

For Reflection: How reasonable are my standards? How do I respond to these standards?

Suggestion: Make a list of everything you plan to do tomorrow. If the list seems too work-oriented, or too play-oriented, add the kind of activity that seems to be lacking: for instance, writing a long overdue letter, or going for a bike ride. If the list seems too long, transfer some of the items to a list for another day. Continue each day to create a balanced plan for the next day.

□□□

Hard as we try to win approval, we seldom handle it well when it does come. We may become embarrassed at the smallest compliment and verbally discount any asset or achievement: "I had a lot of help." "You just can't see where I covered up the mistakes." "It took me longer than it should have." Even if we are able to say a simple "thank you," we may still in our own minds question the taste or intelligence of the person who thinks well of us. We may even feel guilty at having misled that person.

Those of us who fall into the other extreme— bragging about ourselves at every opportunity—are also plagued by low self-esteem. Much as we may brag, we may wonder how long it will be before everyone learns the "truth" about us.

For Reflection: How pleased and how grateful am I for my assets and accomplishments?

Suggestion: Make a list of your assets and accomplishments. If you tend to brag to other people, keep this list to yourself. If you are a self-effacing person, try to read this list to another person, or, if that's too hard, to the family dog or the neighbor's cat.

□□□

Some of us go further than just denying our good qualities. We actually treat ourselves with contempt, endlessly criticizing ourselves: "I act like a child." "How could I say anything so stupid." "I'm so clumsy." "Everyone must have been laughing at the way I was dressed."

The standards we set for ourselves we also set for other people. We are critical, not only of ourselves, but of others. We try to feel better by belittling other people— out loud, or in our thoughts. This may involve major judgments about morality or small criticisms regarding dress or manners.

Judging others, however, may increase our discomfort, since we then begin to suspect that they are judging us in return. When we are criticized, we feel personally attacked, and we have trouble assessing the validity of any negative feedback.

For Reflection: How critical am I of other people—and how sensitive to their criticism of me?

□□□

Having to be perfect also means having to be right. If we get into an argument, we feel we have to win. We may not be the sort of person who winds up winning, but we still feel that need.

We become rigid about our opinions and find it difficult to tolerate disagreement. If people don't agree with us, we feel personally threatened. It is difficult for us to have friends with different beliefs than our own. Within our families, the need is even stronger to have complete agreement. Anything else seems like betrayal.

For Reflection: How important is it for me to be right—and to have others agree with me?

□□□

Against a backdrop of impossibly high standards and absolute right or wrong, we see ourselves as being superior or inferior to others. It is a one-up one-down world. If a friend or family member is "up," we are "down": inadequate and inferior. Being "up" is not a lot better, however, since in that position we are still very much alone.

Up or down, we miss the equality and mutuality that would give us a sense of belonging. By always comparing ourselves to others, by endlessly competing with them, we find it hard to feel close to them. Whether we win or lose the competition, we wind up feeling lonely.

For Reflection: How much does a sense of competition enter into my relationships?

□□□

Some of our desire to get approval is based on our wanting to "fit in." Many of us have grown up feeling that we, or our families, are very different from other people. We seldom feel as though we belong.

Often we feel that we will be accepted only if we hide who we really are. We may go to great lengths to copy what we think is normal and acceptable. We try to look and behave like other people.

Some of us, on the other hand, go to great lengths to be special and unique. We hope to attract people by our dramatically different way of dressing, speaking, or behaving. If we cannot have their love and acceptance, we hope at least to gain their attention.

Whether we are conforming or rebelling, we are playing a role and hiding who we really are. Fearful of discovery, we avoid real intimacy with others. We keep our contacts superficial. We may say little, or we may talk a lot, but we seldom say what we mean or mean what we say.

If we are afraid to have others know us, we are also afraid of getting to know ourselves—fearing, perhaps, that we will not like what we find. We may hide from ourselves by staying busy, absorbed in work or play, or by always managing to have a lot of people around.

For Reflection: Am I able to let others know who I am? Can I be honest with myself?

Suggestion: Sometimes it is easier to be honest, and to learn about ourselves, when we use a medium other than words. Find some colored crayons or pens and draw one picture of yourself at work and another at play. (Don't worry about how "artistic" your creations are.) Tell someone what you think these pictures reveal about you.

□□□

Feeling dependent upon the approval of others, we tend not to act, but to react. Instead of expressing an opinion or taking action based on our own ideas and feelings, we react or respond to the ideas and feelings of other people. We may react not only to what others say and do, but to what we think they are thinking. We can become absorbed in a game of mind-reading.

Sensitive to the feelings of others, we tend to disregard our own feelings. If we hear something that makes us angry or sad, we may continue to smile and carry on the conversation as though nothing has happened. We seldom share our anger or hurt. We worry about expressing any emotion that might cause others to scorn or reject us.

For Reflection: How much am I focused in on what other people are thinking or feeling?

□ □ □

In our attempt to hide from, agree with, and please other people, we may lose sight of what we really think or feel, and eventually, of who we are. We lose our sense of identity.

Although we may lose sight of who we really are, we can be certain that we are clearly known by God. The miracle is that he knows us and *still* accepts us. Because his Son died for us, we are acceptable. Through our relationship with Jesus, we are approved for adoption into the family of God.

Looking at Scripture: Does God know everything about me?

> You know my folly, O God; my guilt is not hidden from you.
>
> PSALM 69:5

> O LORD, you have searched me and you know me. You know when I sit and when I rise; you perceive my thoughts from afar.
>
> PSALM 139:1–2

Looking at Scripture: Does God love me and want me to belong to him in spite of what he knows?

> But God demonstrates his own love for us in this: While we were still sinners, Christ died for us.
>
> ROMANS 5:8

> How great is the love the Father has
> lavished on us, that we should be called
> children of God!
>
> 1 JOHN 3:1

Suggestion: Write a letter to God, your Father, in which you express your sense of inadequacy. Tell him how much you want to have his approval. Ask him to show you that he is pleased with what you try for, that he is happy over each new step of spiritual growth, that he is patient when you fail.

□□□

As we progress in recovery, we become certain of God's acceptance of us. Confident of our standing with him, we become confident when interacting with other people. No longer dependent upon their approval, we are free to move toward them, and free to draw back. This kind of freedom is one of the gifts of recovery.

CHAPTER 7
Hurting for Security

All children need to feel safe and secure. They need to have trust in the people who take care of them. Children who live with unloving, unpredictable, or abusive parents become afraid. To protect themselves, they try to control the mood or behavior of these large and powerful people they are dependent on.

Some children try to manipulate their parents by being obedient, responsible, helpful, and mature. These are the "heroes" who never seem to have a childhood. Others, the "mascots," try to control their parents through their ability to be charming, crack jokes, or play the clown. If being good or being funny doesn't work, a child may become troublesome. Starting arguments, getting into trouble at school are negative ways that "scapegoats" get attention, if not love.

Some children exert control over a bad situation by withdrawing. These are the "lost children"—the quiet, unobtrusive children who protect themselves by disappearing. When they are unable to get away physically, they retreat mentally, into fantasy and daydreams.

For Reflection: Did I try to control my mother or my father? How did I try to do this?

□□□

If we had one parent who hurt us, we probably had another who was unresponsive to our hurt or unable to protect us. As a result, we learned quite early not to trust or depend on others. As adults, we usually continue in our distrust, as well as in our attempts to make our environment safe by trying to control other people.

We may try to control a spouse with sarcasm or with flattery, by withholding sex or by saying yes when we want to say no. We may try to control our children by yelling at or hitting them, or we may give in to their every whim.

Sometimes the methods we use are more subtle and indirect. We may manipulate others by "playing victim" and making them feel guilty, or we may withdraw from them emotionally, in order to have them "chase after" us and give us what we want.

For Reflection: Do I try to control other people? If so, what methods do I use?

□□□

If we need to control others, it is because we are

basically afraid of them. We may be afraid of people we love because they have the power to leave us or hurt us. We may be afraid of authority figures in institutions or in government because they remind us of a powerful and perhaps dangerous parent.

If stopped by a policeman for speeding, some of us will become fearful, apologetic, and ingratiating, while others of us may get very nasty and argumentative. Both reactions, as different as they are, reflect our fear of authority. The rebellion against authority, the need to break or bend the rules, is simply an angry denial of our fear. We find it intolerable to be powerless, to lose control.

For Reflection: Are there people that I am afraid of? How do I deal with these people?

□ □ □

We are often afraid of people who are angry. We may never have learned that anger is an acceptable emotion that can coexist with love and that can be expressed in appropriate ways. We may react to any expression of anger as a very real threat to us, emotionally or physically. In order to avoid even minor arguments, we may continually fail to assert ourselves. Our goal is always to "keep the peace."

Fearing the anger of others, some of us may take the opposite course of action. On the theory that the best defense is a good offense, we may go out of our way to pick fights. We may shout or hit in order to feel safe.

Sometimes we swing between these extremes, "stuffing down" our anger for a long time, and then suddenly exploding. When our anger does erupt, it may take the form of an overpowering, senseless rage against a defenseless child or animal.

For Reflection: How do I deal with anger?

Note: In Chapter 11, you will find some specific guidelines for dealing with anger.

□□□

Sometimes we see being in control as a moral obligation. If we don't manage the world, surely it will all come apart at the seams. Other people just can't be trusted to do the job. As far as we're concerned, other people need a great deal of management—by us, of course.

Our attempts to control other people invariably call for a lot of self-control. We tend to be quite serious and intense about the way we manage our affairs and are concerned about how we are doing at any given moment. Even if we decide to play a life-of-the-party role, we seldom allow ourselves to be completely relaxed or spontaneous. Too much rides on our performance.

For Reflection: How relaxed or spontaneous am I?

□□□

For some of us, the need for security translates to a need for predictability. Usually this causes us to resist change, and to cling to rigid ways of thinking and acting. We stay in jobs or relationships that are counter-productive for us.

Sometimes, however, our fear of change causes us to rush headlong from one thing to another. Always unstable, always unpredictable, we seem to confirm our fear by acting out our most negative expectations.

Because the world seems to be a potentially dangerous place and life seems to be a very serious affair, we may have trouble making decisions. Even a small mistake seems to put us at risk, so even a small decision may be difficult for us. We may delay a decision endlessly, agonizing over the possibility of making a wrong choice.

At other times, our fear makes us impulsive, and we make decisions too quickly. We want immediate grat-ification because we don't trust what tomorrow will bring. Both our indecision and our impulsiveness reveal our lack of security.

For Reflection: How do I deal with decision-making?

Suggestion: To facilitate decision-making, ask God for a knowledge of his will for you. If you do not get a clear idea of what you are to do, tell God you are going to make what seems to be the best choice, and ask him to set up roadblocks to that choice if it is the wrong one for you. Tell him you trust his ability to turn to good any mistake you may make.

□□□

In spite of all that we do to control other people and

protect ourselves against unknown dangers, we are often the most susceptible and vulnerable of people. This is especially true if we have grown up in a potentially violent or dangerous environment.

We seem to have a high tolerance for the inappropriate behavior of others. If a situation creates in us feelings similar to those of childhood, we are apt to accept it. We may repeatedly give another person the "benefit of the doubt," when the behavior of that person is, in fact, unacceptable. Even in adulthood, when we have the power to protect ourselves, we may continue to be abused.

For Reflection: How do I respond to inappropriate or harmful situations?

□□□

Sometimes our fears have a basis in reality—a negative doctor's report, for instance, or a discouraging bank statement. Often, however, our fears are greater than a given situation warrants. We may, in fact, have no reason at all to be fearful.

We may be troubled by a "free-floating" anxiety that seems to hang over us regardless of what is happening in our lives. Or we may be fine most of the time, then suddenly feel an unexplainable surge of fear that leaves as quickly as it came. Perhaps we do not even recognize the uncomfortable feeling we have as being fear.

Life is always unpredictable, often difficult, and sometimes dangerous. Fear in the face of real danger can be helpful, as it prepares our minds and bodies for action. Constant fear when there is no danger robs us of emotional and physical health.

We can live free from constant fear when we trust in God. Certain of his protection and care, we can be optimistic and respond creatively even as we work through problems or face danger. Our safety lies in him.

Looking at Scripture: Is God my ultimate security?

> How priceless is your unfailing love! Both high and low among men find refuge in the shadow of your wings.
>
> PSALM 36:7

> You will keep in perfect peace him whose mind is steadfast, because he trusts in you.
>
> ISAIAH 26:3

> "But blessed is the man who trusts in the LORD, whose confidence is in him. He will be like a tree planted by the water that sends out its roots by the stream. It does not fear when heat comes; its leaves are always green. It has no worries in a year of drought and never fails to bear fruit."
>
> JEREMIAH 17:7–8

> The LORD is with me; I will not be afraid. What can man do to me?
>
> PSALM 118:6

Suggestion: Write a letter to God in which you tell him about your fears—*especially any fear you may have of him*! Tell him you want to trust in his protection, but that you need help to do this.

□□□

As we progress in recovery, we become assured of God's protective care. Feeling safe and secure, we are able to give him control of our lives. We grow relaxed and spontaneous, learning to live each moment fully and to delight in each new day.

CHAPTER 8
Hurting for Understanding

Children feel understood when their feelings are respected and allowed expression. While behavior may be unacceptable, and may need to be controlled, feelings are not right or wrong and they do not need to be controlled. Our feelings, however negative or unpleasant, are the expression of who we are at any given moment.

In a healthy family situation, parents do not try to limit or control how their children feel. In a dysfunctional family, however, children are discouraged from having or verbalizing feelings.

In many cases, children are actually told not to feel a certain way: "You shouldn't feel jealous of your brother." "Don't you speak to me in that angry tone of voice." "Little girls who pout look ugly." "You don't need a drink of water; stop complaining." "If you don't

have something nice to say, don't say anything at all."
"Big boys don't cry."

Children can also become afraid of feelings. In a
family where there is no outlet for feelings, negative
emotions can build to where they are overwhelming. A
father may suddenly break into an unexpected fit of
violent rage. A mother may, for no apparent reason,
sink into a deep depression. These unexplained events
terrify children and teach them they must exert tremendous control over their own feelings—that it is best *not*
to feel.

Sometimes children suppress their feelings when they
are in an unpredictable or unsafe environment. They
adapt to a bad situation by pretending that everything is
fine. They may deny their fear, and they may even deny
that a problem exists. Children can learn to discount or
repress feelings to the point where they finally learn to
stop feeling.

For Reflection: As a child, was I discouraged from
having or expressing certain emotions? If so, which were
denied to me?

□□□

Having learned as children to suppress our feelings,
we may continue, as adults, to be emotionally "shut
down." We may respond to a critical situation by feeling
little or nothing. Days later, we may find ourselves
overreacting to an unrelated and unimportant event.

We may have a number of ways to avoid our feelings. One way may be to focus on other people's problems. Some of us expend tremendous energy worrying about our family members or friends. Absorbed in their pain, we can forget our own problems. Helping them, we can ignore our own need to change and grow.

For Reflection: Do I get caught up in other people's problems?

□□□

Sometimes we minimize our discomfort and distress: "It's not so bad." "It could be worse." "I'm better off than most people." At other times, we completely deny our negative feelings: "It's no problem." "I never get angry." "My marriage is perfect."

It really isn't possible, however, to forget emotional pain. If we deny our negative feelings, pushing them out of our conscious minds, they go to a subconscious level, but they do not go away.

One result of blocking our emotions is that our thinking also becomes blocked. Our energies are spent in trying not to feel, and we cannot focus on the situation at hand with any clarity or insight. In particular, we lose discernment about other people.

Suppressed feelings may also create emotional problems such as depression or a deep sense of estrangement from other people. They may create stress-related physical problems such as hypertension, intestinal problems, or even cancer.

For Reflection: Do I have suppressed feelings that could be causing me emotional or physical problems?

□□□

Sometimes we avoid our feelings through a process of substitution. We create uncomfortable situations for ourselves—minor hurts that distract us from, but also confirm and express, our deeper pain. There are many ways we can make ourselves uncomfortable. Being late is an effective way, since it involves a number of negative emotions such as anxiety, guilt, and feelings of incompetence.

We can also avoid our feelings by creating exciting situations, going from one life-crisis to another. Each crisis gives us a "rush" of adrenalin, and we become as addicted to this substance as we might to any external chemical such as alcohol or drugs.

For Reflection: Is there something about the way I live that keeps me from having to deal with my feelings?

□□□

We use many things besides alcohol or drugs to numb us to our emotional pain. We can become compulsive about overeating or starving; we can become addicted to behaviors such as working, buying, or having sex. We can become dependent on friends, lovers, or members of the family.

All these addictions, compulsions, and dependencies numb our pain. Eventually, however, they only increase our emotional distress. In time, we are less able to see clearly, less willing to confront reality, less willing to work on our real problems. Our low self-esteem drops lower and our sense of guilt increases.

Since personal growth rests on our willingness to be honest, any addiction or compulsion that blocks our thinking and feeling will hold us back in that growth. If you think you may have lost control over a chemical substance or a self-defeating behavior, try now to deal with it.

We all need help in overcoming addictive and compulsive behavior. You can get the help you need from the Twelve-Step approach used by many hospital treatment centers, church fellowships, and all Anonymous groups (Alcoholics Anonymous, Overeaters Anonymous, etc.). A Scriptural approach to the Twelve Steps may be found in the first book of this series, *God, Help Me Stop! Break Free of Addiction and Compulsion.*

For Reflection: Do I have an addiction or compulsion that I use to avoid negative feelings? If so, what am I willing to do about it?

□□□

If we have been emotionally shut down for a long time, we may be afraid of our feelings. We may fear being overwhelmed by them. Basically, this is a fear of losing control: "If I start to cry, I won't ever be able to stop." "If I allow myself to become angry, I may kill someone." "If I get emotional, I may go crazy."

Once acknowledged and expressed, however, feelings do *not* get increasingly out of control. Nor do they last very long. Instead they lose their intensity, become manageable, and dissipate. When we are willing to feel our feelings, we become free of them.

For Reflection: Do I fear losing control of my feelings? What do I think might happen?

□□□

Underneath our feelings of pain and anger are feelings of deep sadness. Ultimately, the sense of being physically or emotionally abandoned as a child leaves us grief-stricken. The emotion we most need to acknowledge, experience, and express is grief. We need to mourn for what we missed as children.

Looking at Scripture: What does Scripture tell me about my grief?

> Sorrow is better than laughter, because a
> sad face is good for the heart. The heart
> of the wise is in the house of mourning,
> but the heart of fools is in the house of
> pleasure.
>
> ECCLESIASTES 7:3–4

> Blessed are those who mourn, for they
> will be comforted.
>
> MATTHEW 5:4

Suggestion: When you pray, place an empty chair across from you and imagine that God is sitting in that chair. Tell him about your feelings.

□□□

When we trust God to accept our feelings, when we trust him to soothe our hurts, dry our tears, and comfort us, we are free to experience fully all our anger, pain, and grief. As we experience these emotions, they teach us who we are and how we can grow. Our most negative emotions are turned by God into gifts of great value by which the "heart is made better."

CHAPTER 9
Hurting for Forgiveness

Children who grow up in dysfunctional families are often burdened with guilt. They feel responsible for the terrible things happening around them. If they are emotionally or physically abused, they assume they must deserve it. If their parents divorce, or if one dies, they assume they are to blame.

Sometimes children are actually told that they are responsible for parental difficulties: "I wouldn't have this heart problem if you didn't get into so much trouble." "You're the reason there's so much friction and argument in this family." "We could go on a vacation if it wasn't for the money we have to spend on your braces."

Parents may also create guilt in children through excessive punishment. Frequent and severe punishment convinces children that they deserve this kind of treatment. Their sense of guilt may also be increased by their reaction to the punishment: imagining how they will "get back at" their parents.

Some parents use religion as a weapon against children, terrorizing them with threats of an angry, punishing God. A five-year-old who is acting like a normal five-year-old, curious and inquisitive about his body and his environment, may be made to feel sinful.

It is not possible for a very young child to have a grasp of morality, to understand the concepts of good and evil. The comprehension of spiritual values is gained slowly, as we mature. Children can grow up feeling that something is terribly wrong with them, that they are inherently bad. Added to their guilt over what they may have done is a deep sense of shame over who they are.

For Reflection: Did I think of myself as a bad child?

□□□

Like other negative emotions of childhood, guilt may be carried into adulthood where it exerts a powerful influence over our behavior. We may not realize, however, how much of what we do is based on guilt. We may not even think of ourselves as feeling guilty.

One reaction to guilt may be to engage in charitable and self-sacrificing behavior within the family, the community, or a larger social framework. When such behavior springs from a love of others and a joy in serving, it benefits both the giver and the receiver. However, when the point of such behavior is to assuage guilt and to punish oneself for past sins, no one may benefit. The person who sacrifices feels resentful and the person who receives may feel under obligation.

Another reaction to feeling guilty is to give up the quest for innocence and accept ourselves as being wicked people. If we decide to play out the role of a "bad" person, we will do so in terms of family judgments. A teenage girl who is called a slut for wanting to date boys may confirm her feelings of guilt by eventually becoming promiscuous. A young boy who is labeled an inconsiderate son may live up to that label in adulthood by ignoring the needs of his elderly parents.

To alleviate our feelings of guilt, we may choose one of the methods above, or we may choose both. Some of us simply alternate between trying for sainthood and being the worst person we can be.

For Reflection: Do I deal with guilt by trying to be very good or by trying to be very bad?

□□□

If we feel a strong sense of guilt, there are many ways in which we may punish ourselves. We may, for instance, push ourselves excessively at work, especially work that is boring, dirty, or strenuous. Some of us simply refrain from pleasure, either avoiding social events and vacations, or sabotaging these happy times with worry, complaining, or quarreling.

We can also punish ourselves by becoming depressed and withdrawing from life. Some of us become chronically ill or accident prone, victims of the stock market or the job market. We may complain bitterly about our "bad luck" without ever understanding that we have, in some cases, chosen these things.

Feelings of guilt may also keep us from standing up for ourselves or taking care of ourselves. We tend to feel responsible for making other people happy rather than for making ourselves happy. We feel uncomfortable when we consider our own needs or desires.

We may be unable to miss church, say "no" to someone's request, or take off from work, even when we have good reason to do any of these things. We expect to be judged and punished. If we do not receive a negative response from others, we judge and punish ourselves with thoughts about how selfish or irresponsible we are.

A strong sense of guilt may keep us in situations that are harmful to us. A woman may remain in a marriage where she is emotionally or physically abused; a man may continue to work for an employer who bullies and takes advantage of him. We stay in such situations because we believe we are supposed to keep hurting, that somehow we do not deserve to be well and happy.

For Reflection: Can I connect any of the negative things in my life with a wish to punish myself?

Suggestion: Make a list of the ways in which you are hard on yourself. Write next to each self-punishing behavior a way of being kind or loving to yourself. Ask God to help you choose the more loving behaviors.

□□□

Sometimes our speech reveals the excessive guilt we feel. We may apologize, saying "I'm sorry," very often during the day, using it as an introductory phrase even when it is inappropriate or unnecessary: "I'm sorry, I didn't hear what you said." "I'm sorry, can you move over a little bit?" "I'm sorry, I need change for this dollar." "I'm sorry, you're standing on my foot."

Another verbal sign of excessive guilt is the constant use of *should* and *shouldn't*: "I should be home making dinner now." "I shouldn't get angry at my wife." "I should visit my parents more often." "I shouldn't be so shy." "I should do better in school." The constant use of these words reinforces a person's sense of moral failure.

Sometimes we apply *should* and *shouldn't* to other people, taking a self-righteous stance toward them. This projection of our guilt onto other people, most often our children, seems to give us some relief. It is a way of telling ourselves that, compared to other people, we aren't so bad after all.

Suggestion: Consider the negative and unnecessary expressions you use on a regular basis. Try to eliminate these from your daily speech.

□□□

As we work toward recovery, we keep in mind that, as small children, we were not in any way responsible for what happened to us. In God's eyes we deserved only love.

Looking at Scripture: How did God see the child that I was?

> "See that you do not look down on one of these little ones. For I tell you that their angels in heaven always see the face of my Father in heaven."
>
> MATTHEW 18:10

> When Jesus saw this, he was indignant. He said to them, "Let the little children come to me, and do not hinder them, for the kingdom of God belongs to such as these." And he took the children in his arms, put his hands on them and blessed them.
>
> MARK 10:14–16

Looking at Scripture: How can I be restored to innocence?

> If we confess our sins, he is faithful and just and will forgive us our sins and purify us from all unrighteousness.
>
> 1 JOHN 1:9

Suggestion: At the end of each day, review both the spiritual successes and failures of that day. Praise God for any growth and ask his forgiveness for any failures. Thank him for his patience and unfailing love.

□□□

Because we are human, it is impossible to live our lives without making mistakes, failing, and sometimes acting in a way that is sinful. In our recovery, however, we find we can accept our humanity because we have an absolute reliance on God's willingness to forgive us. We know he will always restore us to innocence.

PART III

FINDING SOLUTIONS

CHAPTER 10
Growing Free

When we were children, we may have said to ourselves, "When I grow up, I will never be like my mother" or ". . . my father." It often happens, however, that we grow up to be just like our parents. We may treat ourselves, or others (especially our children), just the way our parents treated us.

Turn to the writing exercises you began in Chapter 3. Look at the judgments you made against your parents. Do any of these apply to you? Consider that your "style" may be different, but your attitude the same.

For instance, if your father was given to bragging, you may never brag out loud, yet still find ways of showing off to others. Or, despising yourself for your need to show off, you may be unable to take even well-earned credit for anything. Either way, you are affected by the judgment you made against your father.

Suggestion: Make a list of the ways in which you mirror the judgments made against your parents.

□□□

There is a second way in which we may be affected by these judgments. We may seek out people who are just like our parents and who recreate for us the pain we suffered as children.

In part, we do this because we are convinced that we deserve this kind of treatment. In part, we do this because we keep hoping that this time it will be different; this time the person hurting us will change and behave differently toward us.

Look again at the judgments you made against your parents. Do any of these apply to your spouse? To your best friend? To your boss?

A little girl who finds her father cold and distant will judge him as being unloving. She will struggle to win his love. As an adult, she may continue that struggle with men who are like her father: emotionally unavailable to her. A close, warm, and loving man will not suit her purposes. She is attracted only to those who will challenge her, who will enable her to engage again in her struggle.

For Reflection: How do the judgments I made against my parents influence my attraction to certain people?

□□□

Sometimes we are not aware that we are recreating in

our lives a parent's negative qualities. Sometimes we do know: "I don't want to beat my kids the way my dad beat me, but here I am doing it." "I swore I wouldn't marry a bully like my father, but somehow I did."

As children, we learn from our parents, following the model they provide. As adults, however, we have more sources of knowledge and therefore more options. We know that there are alternative ways of thinking and behaving.

For instance, if a parent taught us to be harsh and critical, we nonetheless understand that the opposite qualities are kindness and praise. Perhaps we even had one parent who exhibited these more positive qualities. Why then do we get locked into the negative qualities? Why are we unable to change the attitudes and behaviors we dislike in ourselves?

It is, perhaps, because of the resentment we continue to carry against the offending parent. The word resentment literally means *a re-feeling*. When we are resentful, we continually re-feel our original anger and re-focus upon our original judgment. This concentration of negative feeling and focus causes us to internalize the very qualities that offend us. Somehow, we wind up living out or living with that which offends us the most.

For Reflection: Do I still feel the hurt and anger that caused me to judge my parents?

□□□

We are not the only ones affected by these judgments.

Our parents are also affected. When we judge our parents, they seem to respond in ways that fulfill our expectations of them. They seem to know what we think of them, and when they are in our presence, they usually behave accordingly.

For Reflection: How do my parents respond to my spoken, or unspoken, judgments of them?

□□□

If we choose to, we can release our parents through prayer from the judgments we have made against them. If we are willing to do this, our parents can be freed from the binding effects of these judgments. What is more, we, too, can be made free of these things.

Once we release our parents, they may sense this, and they may begin to respond to us in surprisingly new ways. Sometimes we can begin to establish a healthier relationship with them.

If our parents have died, we may still, in some sense, begin a new relationship with them. We may feel softened toward them, and more at peace when we think about them.

If our parents are alive, but kept from any change or growth by emotional illness or by problems of addiction, we may still benefit by releasing them from judgment. We may learn to be unaffected by their behavior. Or, if it is necessary to discontinue contact with them, we may be able to do that without guilt or pain.

For Reflection: What do I think might happen if I release my parents from judgment?

□□□

To release our parents from past judgments is not to condone, excuse, or deny what they have done. We do not forget what happened to us, pretend that it never happened, or say that it wasn't important. On the contrary, we remain clear and honest about the wrongs we suffered.

We do, however, separate our understanding of what our parents have done, from what we judge them to be. For instance, we continue to acknowledge that Mother spent more time drinking than caring for her child, but we release her from a judgment such as "selfish" or "disgusting."

Suggestions: Use the following prayer to release your parents from each and every judgment you made against them:

"Lord, I repent of judging my mother (father) as being _____. It was wrong of me to make this judgment. I ask you to forgive me. I ask you to free my parent and myself from the effects of this judgment."

We speak to God about these matters, but we do not speak to our parents. While our parents may know our opinion of them, they may not realize the extent or severity of our judgments, and they could be deeply hurt at hearing these expressed. In addition, bringing up painful episodes from the past might be interpreted as being further attempts to accuse or judge. In defending themselves, they may lash out at us, repeating once again old patterns of abuse.

□□□

Releasing our parents from judgment may be a slow process. It may be experienced in stages, with times when we find ourselves once again angry and critical. These "setbacks" are a normal part of the process. Do not be discouraged. Eventually, as we continue in our recovery, we come to a stage where we not only release our parents from judgment, but we wholeheartedly forgive them.

While such forgiveness is our ultimate goal, it cannot be rushed or forced. It requires a stage of emotional growth that is reached only when we have completed our "feeling work." Until we express our anger, until we feel our hurt and pain, until we grieve for what we missed as children, we are not ready to forgive.

When we have embraced our "ugliest" emotions, we experience ourselves and accept ourselves as we really are: not perfectly good, but not perfectly bad either. We understand that we are simply ordinary people, and somehow we come to accept our parents in the same way.

For the first time, perhaps, we can have compassion for our parents. We see them, not as monsters or as saints, but as human beings with good qualities as well as weaknesses. We see that, underneath their strong exterior, they were as confused or hurting or frightened as they caused us to be. We understand that they, too, were products of their upbringing. We are able to forgive them.

Looking at Scripture: What will it mean to me when I am able to fully forgive my parents?

> Blessed are the merciful, for they will be shown mercy.
>
> MATTHEW 5:7

> "Be merciful, just as your Father is merciful. Do not judge, and you will not be judged. Do not condemn, and you will not be condemned. Forgive, and you will be forgiven. Give, and it will be given to you. A good measure, pressed down, shaken together and running over, will be poured into your lap. For with the measure you use, it will be measured to you."
>
> LUKE 6:36–38

Suggestion: Talk to God honestly about any anger you still hold against your parents. If you are not yet willing to let go of that anger, tell him you are "willing to be willing." Ask him to help bring you to a place of wholehearted forgiveness.

□□□

When we release our parents from the judgments we made against them, we too are released from the binding effects of these judgments. When we have the heart to forgive, we are set free from anger and pain, and we have great peace.

CHAPTER 11
Living Well

Living well, which involves making appropriate choices, usually depends on our having a strong sense of self-worth. Those of us who grew up in dysfunctional homes seldom make appropriate choices because we seldom have confidence in our own value or worth. We may understand, at an intellectual level, that God loves us and that his love gives us value. At an emotional level, however, we tend to question his love and our own self-worth.

As we work toward recovery, we gain some sense of self-worth when we are honest about ourselves with others and find that they accept us just as we are. We also experience self-worth when we forgive our parents and find that we, too, are forgiven and set free.

Still another way to reinforce our sense of self-worth is by being loving toward ourselves. By taking care of ourselves, by treating ourselves with respect, we can confirm our God-given value. Below are some new beliefs and corresponding new attitudes that can help us in this process.

New Belief: Because God loves me, I am an attractive person.

New Attitudes: I do not compare myself to other people, and I do not try to live up to their ideas of what is pleasing or attractive. I thank God for giving me my unique combination of appearance, personality, character, and abilities. When I receive compliments from other people, I accept them graciously.

I do not pretend to be anything I am not. I am honest and open about myself to others. With some people I share my deepest secrets and feelings. I expect people to be attracted to the "real me" and respond with love.

Looking at Scripture:

> I praise you because I am fearfully and wonderfully made; your works are wonderful, I know that full well.
> PSALM 139:14

□□□

New Belief: Because God loves me, I am a loving person.

New Attitudes: I express love for myself by respecting my feelings, opinions, and needs. When I need the help of others, I don't expect them to read my mind. I ask them for what I need or want. Even if they say no, I feel better because I cared enough for myself to ask.

I express love for other people by accepting them just as they are, without trying to change them. I also give to and do things for other people. I can say no, however, to people who would take advantage of me in order to avoid responsibility.

Loving others means that I care about their spiritual growth. Because of this, I do not let people mistreat me. I withdraw from people or situations that are inappropriate or harmful to me.

Looking at Scripture:

> Let us therefore make every effort to do what leads to peace and to mutual edification.
>
> ROMANS 14:19

□□□

New Belief: Because God loves me, I am a valuable person.

New Attitudes: I take good care of my body by eating nutritious meals, getting some exercise, spending some time out-of-doors, and getting enough sleep. I do not abuse my body with chemicals or drugs.

I balance my time to work with time to relax, play, laugh, and do carefree things. I enjoy my own company as well as that of my family and friends. I spend time in prayer and meditation, building my faith in God who loves me, guides me, and supports me through difficult times.

Looking at Scripture:

> He makes me lie down in green pastures,
> he leads me beside quiet waters.
>   PSALM 23:2

□ □ □

New Belief: Because God loves me, I am a peaceful person.

New Attitudes: When I get angry at someone I care about, I express my anger in a way that can lead to reconciliation. I express my feelings without being judgmental or attacking the other person. For instance, I say "I feel imposed upon," rather than "You always get other people to do your work."

If I am unable to handle the situation right away, I wait until I have a chance to get in touch with my feelings (the hurt feelings that are under my anger) by writing a letter that I then throw away, or by talking to someone. If I need to, I work off some emotion physically, by going for a run or punching some pillows.

If I am injured by someone who is emotionally ill, someone who has hurt me out of sheer malice, or someone I don't have the opportunity to speak to, I take my anger to God. Again, I may need to first talk things over with a friend, or express some of my rage in physical ways, but then I am ready to be free of my anger. Even if I have been seriously hurt, I know nothing can separate me from God's love and care. I pray for the ability to forgive, so I can be free of the harmful effects of resentment and bitterness.

Looking at Scripture:

> "In your anger do not sin": Do not let the sun go down while you are still angry, and do not give the devil a foothold.
>
> EPHESIANS 4:26–27

□□□

New Belief: Because God loves me, I am an intelligent person.

New Attitudes: I am interested in learning and I have the ability to understand the world I live in. It is all right for me to say "I don't know" or "I don't understand." I find it easy to ask questions. It is all right for me to be wrong and it is all right for me to change my mind.

I express my opinion even when it differs from the opinion of others. It is not necessary for me to agree with others, even those I love, and it is not necessary for them to agree with me.

If someone offers me advice, I carefully consider it, and then I am free to accept or reject it. If people criticize me, I carefully consider what they have said, and then I am free to decide whether or not their criticism is valid, and whether or not I will choose to make any changes.

Looking at Scripture:

> If any of you lacks wisdom, he should ask God, who gives generously to all without finding fault, and it will be given to him.
>
> JAMES 1:5

□□□

New Belief: Because God loves me, I am a competent person.

New Attitudes: I do not have to earn God's love by being perfect. When I set goals for myself, they are reasonable and reachable. I work toward these with patience.

I congratulate myself on each small accomplishment. When I fail, I congratulate myself on having taken a risk, on having tried. I respond creatively to each mistake or bad decision by accepting it as a positive learning experience. With God's help, I face each new challenge.

Looking at Scripture:

> I can do everything through him who gives me strength.
>
> PHILIPPIANS 4:13

□□□

New Belief: Because God loves me, I am a free
person.

New Attitudes: I live free from guilt. I know that
God, through the sacrifice of his Son, forgives me for
everything I bring to him in repentance. Because Jesus
died for me, I can be cleansed of sin. I am assured of
forgiveness even for the mistakes I will make in the
future. I can therefore learn from the past and look
forward to the future. I can forgive myself.

I can also live free from fear. I do not have to be
afraid of people or situations. I do not have to take life
too seriously. I can sometimes laugh at life and
sometimes laugh at myself.

Giving God control of my life and putting myself in
his hands, I can enjoy living each moment of the day to
its fullest. I do not need an addiction to help me cope
with life. I do not need an addictive "high" to enjoy the
glory and riches of the universe.

Looking at Scripture:

> "Then you will know the truth, and the
> truth will set you free."
> > JOHN 8:32

□□□

To act lovingly toward ourselves is not selfish. Loving
ourselves is what God expects us to do. Understanding

how to love ourselves is, in fact, the basis for knowing
how to love other people, just as our ability to love
ourselves and others affects our ability to love God.

Looking at Scripture: When God asks me to love
him and to love others, does he also expect me to love
myself?

> Jesus replied: "'Love the Lord your God
> with all your heart and with all your soul
> and with all your mind.' This is the first
> and greatest commandment. And the
> second is like it: 'Love your neighbor as
> yourself.'"
>
> MATTHEW 22:37–39

Suggestion: Look into the mirror each day and say
out loud one of the new beliefs given in this chapter.
Write them down and put them where you will see them
often. Add to the list, if you like.

□□□

The love we have for ourselves, the love we have for
God, and the love we have for others are interdependent. To enter into this circular flow of love, at
whatever point, is our ultimate goal. To be in this flow
of love is to be living well.

CHAPTER 12
Feeling Good

We have already taken many steps toward healing and feeling good. We have taken a good, clear look at our problem. We have admitted that, alone, we cannot handle the problem and we have reached out to God and to other people. We have also assumed responsibility for our happiness: instead of judging or blaming our parents, we have worked to correct the way we think and the way we respond to life.

Having done all these things, there is yet one more step to take—one more step to enable us to stop hurting and start feeling good. In the words of the Alcoholics Anonymous program, that is the step of "improving our conscious contact with God." Ultimately, all programs of recovery are spiritual programs. Regardless of whether our problems are physical or emotional, whether they have to do with alcohol or anxiety, the solution for us is always a spiritual one. Feeling good is dependent on our relationship with God.

Improving our relationship with God may be necessary even for those of us who feel we are already
"religious" or "spiritually mature." Even with theologi-
cal studies or regular church attendance, it is possible to
feel emotionally distant from God. Having experienced
a less-than-perfect relationship with less-than-perfect
parents, we may be blocked in our experience of God as
our perfect parent.

We can solve this problem, however, by simply
spending more time with God. When we increase our
contact with him, we learn how good he is, and how
much he loves us.

Looking at Scripture: What will happen if I spend
time with God?

> Taste and see that the LORD is good;
> blessed is the man who takes refuge in
> him.
>
> PSALM 34:8

> "Call to me and I will answer you and tell
> you great and unsearchable things you do
> not know."
>
> JEREMIAH 33:3

□□□

To develop a relationship with God, we use the same
approach we would with another person. We spend time
with him, we are honest and open about our feelings and
ideas, and we listen with interest and respect to what he
has to say.

In some ways it is actually easier to do these things with God than with another person. To begin with, God is always available to us. He always has time for us.

While it is good to set aside a particular time of day to read Scripture, pray, and meditate, we can also have God's company all day long. We can delight in conversation with him while driving a car, participating in a business conference, or washing the kitchen floor. We can have his companionship in the middle of a family celebration or during a long and sleepless night.

Looking at Scripture: Is God always available to me?

> The LORD is near to all who call on him,
> to all who call on him in truth.
>   PSALM 145:18

> You will seek me and find me when you
> seek me with all your heart.
>   JEREMIAH 29:13

> "Ask and it will be given to you; seek and
> you will find; knock and the door will be
> opened to you."
>   MATTHEW 7:7

□□□

Not only is God always there for us, he is easy to talk to. We can be honest with him about our thoughts and feelings. He accepts what we have to say without condemning or rejecting us.

He wants us to be aware of our faults, but not to be discouraged by them. He is never discouraged with us. He is never frustrated or impatient with us, no matter how slow or halting our spiritual progress. When we confess our negative feelings, our foolishness, our fear and shame to him, we are washed clean of all these things.

God is interested in everything we have to say to him. He is never tired of listening. Everything that is important to us is important to him.

Looking at Scripture: Should I talk to God about everything?

> Do not be anxious about anything, but in everything, by prayer and petition, with thanksgiving, present your requests to God.
>
> PHILIPPIANS 4:6

□□□

Although God is always near us, and it is easy for us to talk with him, we may have trouble hearing him. If we have been hurt in the past by ridicule or criticism, we may expect the same kind of negativity from God. As a result, we may be resistant to listening to him. We may miss entirely his words of unconditional love.

Even when reading the Bible, the testament of God's love for us, we may see only those things that leave us feeling discouraged. We may forget that the Gospel is our "good news." We may miss the message of Jesus that he has come to give us sight, to set us free, to heal us of brokenheartedness.

It will take time—time spent with God—for us to hear how sweet his words are. In time, we will recognize his voice in the positive inner promptings we feel. Whether we are reading Scripture, seated in meditation, or running about on some errand, we will begin to hear the soft and loving voice of God reassuring us, encouraging us, guiding us on a sure and steady course.

Looking at Scripture: Can I always rely on God for support and direction?

> "Have I not commanded you? Be strong and courageous. Do not be terrified; do not be discouraged, for the LORD your God will be with you wherever you go."
> JOSHUA 1:9

> If I rise on the wings of the dawn, if I settle on the far side of the sea, even there your hand will guide me, your right hand will hold me fast.
> PSALM 139:9–10

> Whether you turn to the right or to the left, your ears will hear a voice behind you, saying, "This is the way; walk in it."
> ISAIAH 30:21

> For I am convinced that neither death nor life, neither angels nor demons, neither the present nor the future, nor any powers, neither height nor depth,

> nor anything else in all creation, will be
> able to separate us from the love of God
> that is in Christ Jesus our Lord.
>
> ROMANS 8:38–39

Suggestion: Set aside time each day to read from Scripture. Before you begin, ask God to help you understand and trust in his words of love and guidance.

□ □ □

Imagine that you are once again a small child. Perhaps you have an old photo that will help you do this. Picture yourself with your hand in the hand of God. Or imagine yourself asleep, cradled in God's arms, or awake and chatting, sitting on God's lap—or excited and happy, riding on God's shoulders.

These visual images are a representation of spiritual reality. Although you are an adult with an adult's understanding and responsibilities, you are also that loved and cared for child of God.

Looking at Scripture: How important is it for me to understand that I am God's child?

> He called a little child and had him stand
> among them. And he said: "I tell you the
> truth, unless you change and become like
> little children, you will never enter the
> kingdom of heaven. Therefore, whoever
> humbles himself like this child is the
> greatest in the kingdom of heaven."
>
> MATTHEW 18:2–4

Suggestion: Find a photo of yourself from childhood, have it framed, and place it somewhere in your home where you can see it each day. Let it be a reminder to you of your relationship with God.

□□□

When Jesus explained what it meant to believe in him, he used the phrase to be "born again." He spoke of his believers as "children of God," and he himself called God *Abba*, an Aramaic word that translates into English as *Daddy*.

This child-parent relationship with God requires of us that we be humble enough to acknowledge our need for God, and trusting enough to believe he is the perfect parent who is always loving and good to us.

Looking at Scripture: Is God my perfect parent?

> Though my father and mother forsake me, the LORD will receive me.
> > PSALM 27:10

> "Can a mother forget the baby at her breast and have no compassion on the child she has borne? Though she may forget, I will not forget you!"
> > ISAIAH 49:15

> "If you, then, though you are evil, know how to give good gifts to your children, how much more will your Father in

heaven give good gifts to those who ask him!"

MATTHEW 7:11

Every good and perfect gift is from above, coming down from the Father of the heavenly lights, who does not change like shifting shadows.

JAMES 1:17

Suggestion: Memorize one of the verses you liked from this chapter.

□□□

As we improve our relationship with God, we come to know him as the perfect, loving parent we never had. The more we trust him, the more we find him to be trustworthy. The more we depend on him the more we find him to be dependable.

We begin to experience the kingdom of heaven, not only as a future promise, but as a present reality. We feel safe, understood, accepted, and approved of. We feel cherished. We know what it means to be God's beloved child. We have the freedom, peace, and joy that is recovery.

GUIDELINES FOR GROUPS

Meetings

1. If possible, choose a quiet meeting place where there are no distractions such as phone calls or children needing attention. Many churches, banks, and businesses make rooms available to groups free of charge.

2. At the first meeting, give each person a few minutes to explain why he or she has joined the group. Emphasize, though, that no one has to share who does not feel ready to do so. Volunteer to begin by telling your own story. After going around the group, return to anyone who has not spoken and ask gently if he or she is ready to talk yet.

3. You may want to follow the tradition of other self-help groups and have people give their first name only. This tradition helps to underscore the confidentiality of the sharing.

4. During the meeting, members may take turns reading from this book. Any member of the group may then comment on the reading or share a personal response. A chapter may be covered in one meeting, or it may take several meetings, depending on the discussion generated.

5. Begin and end each meeting with prayer, asking the Lord for wisdom and encouragement. You may want

to follow the tradition of other self-help groups and have the group members join hands for the closing prayer.

6. Meetings should start and end promptly. One to one-and-a-half hours should be sufficient. Allow time at the end of the meeting for any necessary business.

7. Avoid discussion of religious or denominational differences, of various kinds of therapies, or of other issues that could result in debate or divisiveness.

8. Do not allow eating, smoking, or drinking during the meeting as these distract from the business at hand and may be a problem for compulsive overeaters or people with addictions to nicotine or caffeine.

9. Provide the group with a list of members' names and phone numbers, and encourage people to call one another during the week for "mini-meetings."

10. Some members may benefit from attending more than one meeting a week. They can be encouraged to join an Adult Children of Alcoholics group.

11. If your group begins to grow beyond ten or twelve members, you may want to start a second group. Small groups are best because they encourage an intimate level of sharing and everyone gets a chance to share.

12. When you have finished going through this book, you may want to begin again with Chapter 1. As

GUIDELINES FOR GROUPS   113

you study the material again, you may find yourself relating to it at a new and deeper level. It is often difficult for us to understand and accept certain ideas until we are progressing in our recovery.

Group Interaction

The guidelines that follow will help create an environment of trust, safety, and support in your group. They should be read aloud, and discussed, at the first meeting. It will also be helpful to review them occasionally, especially if new members join after the group has started.

1. Assure Confidentiality: Everything we hear in our meetings should be kept confidential. No member of this group is ever discussed outside of this group, not even with another group member. Our healing is dependent on the trust we have in one another, and the freedom we feel to share openly and honestly, without fear of exposure outside of the meetings.

2. Avoid Cross-talk: Cross-talk is talking to another person about their problems rather than discussing our own. It is all right to refer briefly to what another person has said, but each of us needs to talk about our own experiences, feelings, or problems. For instance: "I felt upset when you talked about your father hitting you, because last week I . . ." We must be especially careful to avoid cross-talk that involves criticism, advice, or denial of another person's pain.

a. Criticism: If we feel criticized or judged, our response will be to stop sharing, and we will experience an increased sense of guilt, hopelessness, and isolation. We need to be free to admit certain personal negative things knowing that the response of the group will be loving acceptance. (The only exception to the "no criticism" rule is when a member says or does something that violates the guidelines of this group. Such behavior is subject to discussion and group decision.)

b. Advice: We tend to resist advice, often because it leaves us feeling "talked down to." Sometimes we feel that the advice is given without understanding or sympathy for the particulars of our personality, our history, and our situation. Even when we know the advice to be good, we may feel powerless to follow it. As a result, even good advice may leave us feeling hopeless. We are able to learn and grow from receiving love, support, and acceptance and from seeing others getting well. What we share here is not advice, but our own experience, strength, and hope.

c. Denial of Negative Emotions: It is important that each of us feels free to express negative emotions such as pain, grief, or anger. Much compulsive behavior is the result of not being "in touch with" our feelings or of being afraid to acknowledge or express those feelings. We should never cut another person off with a statement such as, "You're forgetting the Lord can bring good out of this," or "You have to have faith that this will work out." Such statements are true, but they are not helpful when used to cut a person off from expressing feelings. If anything, they create more distress by their implication that the person suffering is lacking in faith and is somehow not a good Christian. When our feelings are discounted we feel invalidated. We stop sharing our feelings, and we lose all hope of working through and being freed from our pain.

Leadership

Being a group discussion leader does not require professional training. You are not expected to have all the answers. You are not asked to teach. If you are willing to work on your own problems, if you do so with honesty, humility, and vulnerability, you will set the best possible example for the group.

Being a group leader does not mean you are responsible for anyone's getting well. Recovery from compulsive behavior is a difficult process that can often take a very long time, and that may be marked by severe setbacks or relapses. It is not your job to correct, improve, or heal anyone. That is the job of the Lord, and he works when we are ready and willing for him to do so.

To sum up, the leader's job is not to teach or to heal, but to serve. There are three ways to serve your group:

1. Help provide a loving, trusting environment.

2. Maintain a balance between time spent reading from this book and time spent in sharing.

3. Work on your own problems.

4. Pray for the members of your group during the week.

Ideally, leadership should be rotated with each meeting, so that all members share this service.

OTHER RESOURCES

Whether or not there was any abuse of alcohol in your family of origin, you may wish to look into the activities of Adult Children of Alcoholics (ACA) groups and the related literature. Most ACA groups include people from all kinds of dysfunctional families. You may find information about local ACA groups from local Alcoholics Anonymous and Al-Anon groups. Check your telephone book for these numbers, or contact:

> National Association for Children of Alcoholics
> 31706 Coast Highway, Suite 201
> South Laguna, CA 92677-3044
> (714) 499-3044

The literature relating to adult children of alcoholics is easily applied to adult children from any dysfunctional family. Your local bookstore may carry a number of these books. The following books are particularly recommended as guides to recovery:

Kritsberg, W. *The Adult Children of Alcoholics Syndrome: From Discovery to Recovery.* Pompano Beach, Fla.: Health Communicators, 1985.

Gravitz, H. L., and Bowden, J. D. *Recovery: A Guide for Adult Children of Alcoholics.* New York, N.Y.: Simon and Schuster, 1985.

Also by Claire W.

GOD, HELP ME STOP!
Break Free from Addiction and Compulsion

Here is a presentation of the Twelve Steps of Alcoholics Anonymous as applied to any addictive or compulsive behavior: alcoholism, overeating, smoking, compulsive gambling, sexual addiction, etc. Verses from the Bible illuminate each step of emotional and spiritual healing. Includes the author's personal story of recovery.

"We have used *God, Help Me Stop!* in a group therapy context, as well as for clients in individual therapy, and it is very helpful in both settings. Thank you for your part in such a practical, Christian approach to the problems of dependency and addiction."

—*Ruth Blight, Counselor*
Counseling Group, Burnmady, B.C.

"*God, Help Me Stop!* has really helped me in my struggle against alcoholism—I've been sober three months now. Thank you for a wonderful tool to work with."

—*V.C., New Boston, MI*

"As one involved in health ministry, I recommend this workbook to those in the pastoral ministry, as well as anyone working with clients who are ready to take the first step to recovery."

—*Stoy Proctor*
Ministry: International Journal for Clergy

Books by Claire W. are available in both book and workbook format. You may buy books at your local Christian bookstore or by calling 1-800-727-3480. To order workbooks, please see order form at back of book.

Also by Claire W.

GOD, WHERE IS LOVE?
Break Free from the Pain of Codependency

For singles or marrieds who struggle with the effects of codependency, here is a guide for improving relationship and communication skills. A comparison between addictive and healthy relationships, personal questions for reflection and Biblical references promote understanding, healing, and growth.

"Ever looked for a missing piece in your puzzle and finally found it? That's how I felt after reading *God, Where Is Love?* This book completes the recovery/healing/growth process that started with Claire W.'s first two books. It is all that it declares itself to be—a guide to helping God's children feel loved by others and by the Lord himself. We have used the other books with good success and I am sure *God, Where Is Love?* is going to be just as important to our expanding program."

—*Dave Carder, Assistant Pastor*
Counseling Ministry, First Evangelical Free Church
Fullerton, CA

"Claire W. has brilliantly penetrated to the heart of what is troubling many marriages today. For married couples who are finding it difficult to communicate with each other, she offers an adjustment built on love, mutual respect, and personal freedom. A very helpful book that will bring hope to many in deep need."

Sherwood E. Wirt, editor emeritus
Decision magazine

Also by Claire W.

GOD, HELP ME CREATE
Realize Your Creative Potential

Whether you want to start a business or write a novel
. . . design a building or develop a hybrid rose . . . here
is a simple, Bible-based guide to help you start, keep at,
and complete the creative project of your choice.

"Claire W. challenges the raw gems of creativity that lie buried
within us. Like a diamond cutter, she uses her gentle, precise words
to carve out potential, chip away at flawed thinking and motives,
and help us to uncover and enjoy the many facets of our God-given
abilities. Those of us who have worked our way through these pages
have increased in value."

—Susan Lenzkes, Author and Lecturer
San Diego, CA

"Here, our secrets are exposed, our dreams revealed, our failures
forgiven, and our gifting affirmed and channeled."

—Judith Dupree, Poet
La Mesa, CA

Books by Claire W. are available in both book and workbook format.
You may buy books at your local Christian bookstore or by calling 1-800-
727-3480. To order workbooks, please see order form at back of book.

ORDER FORM

The God Help Me Series
is also available in the following formats:
Workbooks: 8½" x 11", with space to enter Scriptures and comments.
Audio Tape Sets: 2 tapes, 2 to 3 hours listening time, unabridged text.

	Workbooks	Tape Sets
GOD, HELP ME STOP!	_____	_____
GOD, I'M STILL HURTING	_____	_____
GOD, WHERE IS LOVE?	_____	_____
GOD, HELP ME CREATE	_____	_____

Total Number of workbooks _____ @ $12.95 $_____

Total Number of tape sets _____ @ $14.95 $_____

Shipping and Handling on first item $ 4.00
      on _____ additional items @ 50¢ each $_____

Sales Tax only on shipments to California: 7.25%
      (San Diego County: 7.75%) $_____

                                    TOTAL $_____

Method of Payment:

[   ] Check or money order to Books West

[   ] Visa   [   ] MasterCard

Card # | | | | | | | | | | | | | | | | |

Expires | | | | |

Signature _____

VISA/MasterCard Phone Orders: 1-800-253-8641

Name _____ Phone _____

Organization _____

Street _____

City_____ State_____ Zip_____

BOOKS WEST / P.O. BOX 27364 / SAN DIEGO, CA 92198